Peace

Christian Living in a Violent World

Mary I. Farr

Augsburg Fortress, Minneapolis

Contents

INTERSECTIONS
Small Group Series

Peace
Christian Living in a Violent World

Developed in cooperation with the Division for Congregational Ministries

George W. Johnson, series introduction
David W. Anderson and Carolyn F. Lystig, editors
The Wells Group, series design
Ed Harp/Unicorn Stock Photos, cover photo

Scripture quotations are from New Revised Standard Version Bible, copyright 1989 Division of Christian Education of the National Council of the Churches of Christ in the United States of America. Used by permission.

Copyright © 1995 Augsburg Fortress
All rights reserved. May not be reproduced.
ISBN 0-8066-0135-3
Printed on 50% recycled paper (10% postconsumer fibers)
Manufactured in U.S.A.

1 2 3 4 5 6 7 8 9 0 1 2 3 4 5 6 7 8 9

Introduction

Troubled times

We live in troubled times. Violent times. We secure our doors and secure our parking lots. We install security fences, and we watch the news that tells us we need even more personal protection.

We feel fragile and vulnerable, yearning for God's presence. We long for God to deliver us and make life safe.

Pursuing harmony

Peace: Christian Living in a Violent World offers guidance, hope, and a way of life for those who long for peace.

The biblical understanding of peace serves as the cornerstone for a way of faithful living that encourages us to examine our daily lives as we pursue harmony and wholeness.

- How do we already experience peace and wholeness in our communities and homes?

- Where do we feel broken and incomplete?

- How can we nurture peacemaking in our neighborhoods, with those we love, and in our churches?

This small group study is an occasion to learn and speak peace in simple, practical, and sometimes provocative ways.

Shalom

The first of six chapter themes begins with a study of *shalom*, the Old Testament word for peace, peace as a gift of God.

We experience shalom as an act of God's graciousness in our lives. More than an absence of conflict, shalom plays a vital role in building and protecting the well-being of all our communities, large and small.

We receive this gift of peace as a sign of God's active presence and caring. We offer it to one another in many ordinary yet meaningful ways such as hospitality, listening, affirmation, and acceptance.

God's grace

Chapter 2 looks at peace as an experience of God's healing grace. The fundamental question "Do we want to be healed?" underlies this section.

The discussion and exercises touch issues such as being at peace and the role of pain in our journey toward wholeness. Love as a commitment rather than emotion opens the door to discussion about love's relationship to peace.

Within the faith community

Peace within the faith community provides the focus for chapter 3. Community life grounded on God's forgiveness and reconciliation is the basis for our experience of peace.

To speak about the dark side of humanity is to speak of feelings of fear, humiliation, anger, helplessness, violation, and depression. Verbal, emotional, physical, and sexual violence beget violence. Violence of any sort attacks God's design for peace.

We will take the opportunity to survey our homes, neighborhoods, and church for evidence of peace, justice, and courage in relationships.

Resolving differences

Chapter 4 asks us to probe the ways we resolve our differences. Shalom implies a conversion of hostility to an energy of compassion and justice.

We will talk about hope and loss of hope. We will also review our culture with its gifts of freedom as well as its penchant for rugged individualism.

- What do we mean when we speak of *divinity?*
- How can we gain a sense of harmony through our ability to appreciate the sacramental value of the ordinary?

Shalom in nature

The vision of shalom in all of nature invites the people of God to be sensitive to issues of ecology and the created order. Chapter 5 includes biblical texts that can imply (correctly or incorrectly) our right to dominion over nature. Have we used this as an excuse to abuse our environment?

The prophet Isaiah's picture of a radically different social order becomes the backdrop for a discussion about ideals.

- Are ideals and values important?
- How can we establish ideals for ourselves and our children?

Servanthood

Chapter 6 wraps the series up with the subject of peace as a way of life, not simply a concept to be learned. To fully experience God's gift of enduring life and wholeness, we must lay aside countless human attitudes about prosperity and success. Money is power. Information is power. Silence is power. Food is power.

In what ways do we manipulate our way into positions of power against one another? In fact, it is servanthood and humility, not power, that ultimately allow us to build peace in our lives.

Daily peacemaking tasks

The subject matter and small group setting will provide a safe place for us to rethink the meaning of biblical peace, or shalom, in our own lives. Our use of language and our understanding of words such as *justice, humanity,* and *sacrament* play a significant role in the way we think about shalom.

Problem-solving with our children, coexisting peacefully with partners whose ideas and opinions conflict with ours—these are things that comprise the peacemaking tasks we face each day.

In the ordinary

Finally, we learn that God is always pursuing us. God is with us. God appears in the ordinary, in the mustard seed, and in the bread. We don't need to look for the extraordinary to find shalom. We need to discover the potential for peacemaking and peace in each day's events and especially in the ways we touch one another's lives.

We discover the potential for peace when we reexamine and reorder our attitudes and ambitions, our relationships and our ideals.

God's answer, then, to our fear and vulnerability in these troubled times is solidarity with us. We cannot escape the human condition, but we can count on a God who will be with us and whose loving presence will triumph.

SMALL GROUP SERIES

Welcome into the family of those who are part of small groups! Intersections Small Group Series will help you and other members of your group build relationships and discover ways to connect the Christian faith with your everyday life.

This book is prepared for those who want to make a difference in this world, who want to grow in their Christian faith, as well as for those who are beginning to explore the Christian faith. The information in this introduction to the Intersections small group experience can help your group make the most out of your time together.

Biblical encouragement

"Do not be conformed to this world, but be transformed by the renewing of your minds, so that you may discern what is the will of God—what is good and acceptable and perfect" (Romans 12:2).

Small groups provide an atmosphere where the Holy Spirit can transform lives. As you share your life stories and learn together, God's Spirit can work to enlighten and direct you.

Strength is provided to face the pressures to conform to forces and influences that are opposed to what is "good and acceptable and perfect." To "be transformed" is an ongoing experience of God's grace as we take up the cross and follow Jesus. Changed lives happen as we live in community with one another. Small groups encourage such change and growth.

What is a small group?

A number of definitions and descriptions of the small group ministry experience exist throughout the church. Roberta Hestenes, a Presbyterian pastor and author, defines a small group as an intentional face-to-face gathering of three to twelve people who meet regularly with the common purpose of discovering and growing in the possibilities of the abundant life.

Whatever definition you use, the following characteristics are important.

Small—Seven to ten people is ideal so that everyone can be heard and no one's voice is lost. More than 12 members makes genuine caring difficult.

Intentional—Commitment to the group is a high priority.

Personal—Sharing experiences and insights is more important than mastering content.

Conversational—Leaders that facilitate conversation, rather than teach, are the key to encouraging participation.

Friendly—Having a warm, accepting, non-judgmental atmosphere is essential.

Christ-centered—The small group experience is biblically based, related to the real world, and founded on Christ.

Features of Intersections Small Group Series

A small group model

A number of small group ministry models exist. Most models include three types of small groups:

- *Discipleship groups*—where people gather to grow in Christian faith and life;

- *Support and recovery groups*—which focus on special interests, concerns, or needs; and

- *Ministry groups*—which have a task-oriented focus.

Intersections Small Group Series presently offers material for discipleship groups and support and recovery groups.

For discipleship groups, this series offers a variety of courses with Bible study at the center. What makes a discipleship group different from traditional group Bible studies? In discipleship groups, members bring their life experience to the exploration of the biblical material.

For support and recovery groups, Intersections Small Group Series offers topical material to assist group members in dealing with issues related to their common experience, hurt, or interest. An extra section of facilitator helps in the back of the book will assist leaders of support and recovery groups to anticipate and prepare for special circumstances and needs that may arise as group members explore a topic.

Ministry groups can benefit from an environment that includes prayer, biblical reflection, and relationship building, in addition to their task focus.

Four essentials

Prayer, personal sharing, biblical reflection, and a group ministry task are part of each time you gather. These are all important for Christian community to be experienced. Each of the six chapter themes in each book includes:

- Short prayers to open and close your time together.

- Carefully worded questions to make personal sharing safe, non-threatening, and voluntary.

- A biblical base from which to understand and discover the power and grace of God. God's Word is the compass that keeps the group on course.

- A group ministry task to encourage both individuals and the group as a whole to find ways to put faith into action.

Flexibility

Each book contains six chapter themes that may be covered in six sessions or easily extended for groups that meet for a longer period of time. Each chapter theme is organized around two to three main topics with supplemental material to make it easily adaptable to your small group's needs. You need not use all the material. Most themes will work well for 1½- to 2-hour sessions, but a variety of scheduling options is possible.

Bible based

Each of the six chapter themes in the book includes one or more Bible texts printed in its entirety from the New Revised Standard Version of the Bible. This makes it easy for all group members to read and learn from the same text. Participants will be encouraged through questions, with exercises, and by other group members to address biblical texts in the context of their own lives.

User friendly

The material is prepared in such a way that it is easy to follow, practical, and does not require a professional to lead it. Designating one to be the facilitator to guide the group is important, but there is no requirement for this person to be theologically trained or an expert in the course topic. Many times options are given so that no one will feel forced into any set way of responding.

Group goals and process

1. Creating a group covenant or contract for your time together will be important. During your first meeting, discuss these important characteristics of all small groups and decide how your group will handle them.

Confidentiality—Agreeing that sensitive issues that are shared remain in the group.

Regular attendance—Agreeing to make meetings a top priority.

Non-judgmental behavior—Agreeing to confess one's own shortcomings, if appropriate, not those of others, and not giving advice unless asked for it.

Prayer and support—Being sensitive to one another, listening, becoming a caring community.

Accountability—Being responsible to each other and open to change.

Items in your covenant should be agreed upon by all members. Add to the group covenant as you go along. Space to record key aspects is included in the back of this book. See page 60.

2. Everyone is responsible for the success of the group, but do arrange to have one facilitator who can guide the group process each time you meet.

The facilitator is not a teacher or healer. Teaching, learning, and healing happen from the group experience. The facilitator is more of a shepherd who leads the flock to where they can feed and drink and feel safe.

Remember, an important goal is to experience genuine love and community in a Christ-centered atmosphere. To help make this happen, the facilitator encourages active listening and honest sharing. This person allows the material to facilitate opportunities for self-awareness and interaction with others.

Leadership is shared in a healthy group, but the facilitator is the one designated to set the pace, keep the group focused, and enable the members to support and care for each other.

People need to sense trust and freedom as the group develops; therefore, avoid "shoulds" or "musts" in your group.

3. Taking on a group ministry task can help members of your group balance personal growth with service to others.

In your first session, identify ways your group can offer help to others within the congregation or in your surrounding community. Take time at each meeting to do or arrange for that ministry task. Many times it is in the doing that we discover what we believe or how God is working in our lives.

4. Starting or continuing a personal action plan offers a way to address personal needs that you become aware of in your small group experience.

For example, you might want to spend more time in conversation with a friend or spouse. Your action plan might state, "I plan to visit with Terry two times before our next small group meeting."

If you decide to pursue a personal action plan, consider sharing it with your small group. Your group can be helpful in at least three ways: by giving support; helping to define the plan in realistic, measurable ways; and offering a source to whom you can be accountable.

5. Prayer is part of small group fellowship. There is great power in group prayer, but not everyone feels free to offer spontaneous prayer. That's okay.

Learning to pray aloud takes time and practice. If you feel uncomfortable, start with simple and short prayers. And remember to pray for other members between sessions.

Use page 61 in the back of this book to note prayer requests made by group members.

6. Consider using a journal to help reflect on your experiences and insights between meeting times.

Writing about feelings, ideas, and questions can be one way to express yourself; plus it helps you remember what so often gets lost with time.

The "Daily Walk" component includes material that can get your journaling started. This, of course, is up to you and need not be done on any regular schedule. Even doing it once a week can be time well spent.

How to use this book

The material provided for each session is organized around some key components. If you are the facilitator for your small group, be sure to read this section carefully.

The facilitator's role is to establish a hospitable atmosphere and set a tone that encourages participants to share, reflect, and listen to each other. Some important practical things can help make this happen.

- Whenever possible meet in homes. Be sure to provide clear directions about how to get there.

- Use name tags for several sessions.

- Place the chairs in a circle and close enough for everyone to hear and feel connected.

- Be sure everyone has access to a book; preparation will pay off.

Welcoming

A welcoming atmosphere for these sessions could begin with "peaceful" music to help people relax and focus on the small group experience. Invite group members to bring music selections, and start each session with a few minutes of reflection. Follow this with a renewed commitment to keeping the group's discussions confidential.

The climate created as people arrive for the small group is important to the content of the biblical review itself. We embody biblical shalom by the ways we receive—or do not receive—others. Keep distractions to a minimum so that a genuine sense of hospitality pervades the group.

The goal is for everyone to experience *shalom*, the divine presence that breathes peace, acceptance, renewal, and belonging. It is a power and an experience that you will want for every moment of your life.

By greeting one another with words, actions, and a general environment of shalom, people can feel free to reflect and to share, and will be empowered to grow in their Christian journey as individuals and as a community.

chapter themes in this book
us statement. Read it aloud.
veryone a sense of the direc-
n session and provide some
s so that people will not feel lost
ated trying to cover everything.
us also connects the theme to the
e topic.

Community building

This opening activity is crucial to a re-laxed, friendly atmosphere. It will prepare the ground for gradual group develop-ment. Two "Community Building" options are provided under each theme. With the facilitator giving his or her response to the questions first, others are free to follow.

One purpose for this section is to allow everyone to participate as he or she re-sponds to non-threatening questions. The activity serves as a check-in time when participants are invited to share how things are going or what is new.

Make this time light and fun; remember, humor is a welcome gift. Use 15 to 20 min-utes for this activity in your first few ses-sions and keep the entire group together.

During your first meeting, encourage group members to write down names and phone numbers (when appropriate) of the other members, so people can keep in touch. Use page 59 for this purpose.

Discovery

This component focuses on exploring the theme for your time together, using mater-ial that is read, and questions and exercises that encourage sharing of personal insights and experiences.

Reading material includes a Bible text with supplemental passages and commentary written by the topic writer. Have volun-teers read the Bible texts aloud. Read the commentary aloud only when it seems helpful. The main passage to be used is printed so that everyone operates from a common translation and sees the text.

"A Further Look" is included in some places to give you additional study mater-ial if time permits. Use it to explore related passages and questions. Be sure to have your own Bible handy.

Questions and exercises related to the theme will invite personal sharing and sto-rytelling. Keep in mind that as you listen to each other's stories, you are inspired to live more fully in the grace and will of God. Such exchanges make Christianity relevant and transformation more likely to happen. Caring relationships are key to clarifying one's beliefs. Sharing personal experiences and insights is what makes the small group spiritually satisfying.

Most people are open to sharing their life stories, especially if they're given permis-sion to do so and they know someone will actively listen. Starting with the facilita-tor's response usually works best. On some occasions you may want to break the group into units of three or four persons to explore certain questions. When you recon-vene, relate your experience to the whole group. The phrase "Explore and Relate," which appears occasionally in the margin, refers to this recommendation. Encourage couples to separate for this smaller group activity. Appoint someone to start the dis-cussion.

Wrap-up

Plan your schedule so that there will be enough time for wrapping up. This time can include work on your group ministry task, review of key discoveries during your time together, identifying personal and prayer concerns, closing prayers, and the Lord's Prayer.

The facilitator can help the group identify and plan its ministry task. Introduce the idea and decide on your group ministry task during "Wrap-up" time in the first session. Tasks need not be grandiose. Activities might include:

- Ministry in your community, such as "adopting" a food shelf, clothes closet, or homeless shelter; sponsoring equipment, food, or clothing drives; or sending members to staff the shelter.

- Ministry to members of the congregation, such as writing notes to those who are ill or bereaved.

- Congregational tasks where volunteers are always needed, such as serving refreshments during the fellowship time after worship, stuffing envelopes for a church mailing, or taking responsibility for altar preparations for one month.

Depending upon the task, you can use part of each meeting time to carry out or plan the task.

In the "Wrap-up," allow time for people to share insights and encouragements and to voice special prayer requests. Just to mention someone who needs prayer is a form of prayer. The "Wrap-up" time may include a brief worship experience with candles, prayers, and singing. You might form a circle and hold hands. Silence can be effective. If you use the Lord's Prayer in your group, select the version that is known in your setting. There is space on page 62 to record the version your group uses. Another closing prayer is also printed on page 62. Before you go, ask members to pray for one another during the week. Remember also any special concerns or prayer requests.

Daily walk

Seven Bible readings and a thought, prayer, and verse for the journey related to the material just discussed are provided for those who want to keep the theme before them between sessions. These brief readings may be used for devotional time. Some group members may want to memorize selected passages. The Bible readings can also be used for supplemental study by the group if needed. Prayer for other group members can also be part of this time of personal reflection.

A word of encouragement

No material is ever complete or perfect for every situation or group. Creativity and imagination will be important gifts for the facilitator to bring to each theme. Keep in mind that it is in community that we are challenged to grow in Jesus Christ. Together we become what we could not become alone. It is God's plan that it be so.

For additional resources and ideas see *Starting Small Groups—and Keeping Them Going* (Minneapolis: Augsburg Fortress, 1995).

1 Peace: A Gift of God

Focus

Shalom, or biblical peace, goes beyond nonviolence to God's active care, which leads us to wholeness, harmony, and a sense of well-being.

Community building

The peace of God dwells within the simple, mundane events of our daily lives together. These events include our commitment to one another in this group, our obligation to arrive on time and to protect and respect one another's confidences.

For setting small group goals, see page 7.

More than an absence of conflict, the peace that we will explore is ours as a gift of grace, a powerful presence of God that overcomes fear and despair. It plays a vital role in the creation and nurturing of all our communities.

List your goals and commitments in the appendix on page 60 for future reference.

- Begin by introducing yourselves and sharing one thing each of you hopes to gain from this small group experience on peace.

- Identify individual and group goals and commitments.

- Discuss the value of a group ministry task and some possible task options.

- Conclude your goal-setting and affirm your commitment to each other by using the words of Jesus, "Peace be with you" (John 20:19), as a greeting to one another.

Option

Which of the following is the most/least used depiction of peace in magazines, newspapers, and other media? Explain.

Romantic love
Rewards and wealth
Non-violence
Feeling good
Escaping
Responsible living
A religious concept

Opening prayer

O God, source of all goodness and truth, help us to grow in wisdom and knowledge of your gift of peace. Direct us in our daily affairs toward a place of healing and trust. Amen.

John 14:27

²⁷ **Peace I leave with you; my peace I give to you. I do not give to you as the world gives. Do not let your hearts be troubled, and do not let them be afraid.**

Preparation

As Jesus prepares his disciples for his departure from them just prior to his crucifixion, he expresses a deep concern for his friends. He repeats his earlier urging, "Do not let your hearts be troubled" (John 14:1). So, it is peace, not trouble and worry, that he proposes to leave with them.

Even as he faces his death, Jesus meets the disciples' anxiety with the promise of his coming. They can trust him to return. Given the dramatic conditions, he also possesses a sense of peace that seems unimaginable in its scope. This is clearly a kind of peace that exceeds anything the world might have to offer. Further, he does not just lecture his disciples about this peace, he offers it to them as an unexpected gift.

Shalom

When Jesus speaks of peace, he is tapping into his rich Jewish heritage that speaks of *shalom,* the Hebrew word for peace. Shalom has little to do with satisfaction gained from worldly possessions or personal achievements. God's will for life, love, and mercy define biblical peace.

Discuss as a group.

■ Which expression of shalom do you want to give more attention in your life? Explain.

   a. An expectation that life is good and meaningful.
   b. The ability to safely encounter daily life without being overwhelmed by its difficulties.
   c. A contentment that the pleasures and securities of the world cannot give.
   d. Counting on God's presence to carry us through upheaval, unfairness, and shattered dreams.
   e. The freedom to look at each day as filled with promise and possibility rather than limitations.
   f. Defining health fundamentally as living with the steadfast and saving love of God.

Much as we sincerely strive to find peace within our hearts, we all experience the bitterness of disappointment, failure, and defeat. Imagine Jesus standing before you and saying, "Peace I leave with you. . . . Do not let your hearts be troubled."

■ Identify an area of your life that those words address with particular meaning.

Choose one and explain.

a. Family relationships   e. Job satisfaction
b. Neighborhood violence   f. Personal health
c. Concern for global peace g. Other
d. Personal relationship
   with God

Acceptance

In Philippians 4:11-13, Paul speaks of his acceptance of what is. "Not that I am referring to being in need; for I have learned to be content with whatever I have" (4:11). Paul's words are often in contrast with our inability or unwillingness to accept life with limits. What about all those things we would like to change? That *need* to change?

■ In your experience, which of the following best conveys acceptance? What else conveys acceptance?

a. Going with the flow   c. Tolerating everything
b. Assuming a passive   d. Looking for meaning
   stance toward life   in all things

A gift of God

As a biblical term, peace stands with other biblical ideas such as justice, truth, love, righteousness, and salvation. This kind of peace is a gift of God (Psalm 29:11; Proverbs 3:17).   *Me*

Consider the countless ways in which we might share that gift with others whose lives merge with our own. For example, some gifts of peace we each bring to our daily encounters include hospitality, listening, affirmation, acceptance, tenderness.

■ Share the last time you offered one of these to someone.

■ When did someone last offer one to you?

■ Describe the outcome of those experiences.

Explore and relate.
Explore in groups of three or four; then *relate* a brief summary to the entire group. See page 9 for further explanation.

Consider this

We are ultimately called not to achieve or attain, but to walk with Christ on the holy ground of our human experience—the ordinary, plain, and sometimes painful experiences of living open to the presence of God (Proverbs 11:2). Our daily lives provide the meeting place where we en-

encounter biblical shalom. They are places of God's revelations through which we become increasingly aware of our need for healing and for joy.

■ If shalom means harmony and well-being, in which of the following do you already find peace?

a. Listening to a child
b. Preparing meals
c. Being with a friend
d. Meditating and praying
e. Watching the sunrise
f. Other

A further look

Explore and relate.

Read Psalms 40:4; 84:12; Proverbs 16:20; Jeremiah 17:7.

■ What does it mean to fully trust another?

■ What kind of responsibility does that place on the person who receives that trust?

■ What do you see as the biggest barriers to trusting?

■ Can you think of times when you have completely trusted God? Was it by choice or by circumstances?

Discovery

If this study theme is used for more than one small group session, introduce subsequent sessions with a "Community Builder" and "Opening Prayer" and end with "Wrap-up."

John 16:32-33

32 The hour is coming, indeed it has come, when you will be scattered, each one to his home, and you will leave me alone. Yet I am not alone because the Father is with me. 33 I have said this to you, so that in me you may have peace. In the world you face persecution. But take courage; I have overcome the world!

Confusion

We are
Re-shaped by circum-
- under control
X - not under
control
Re-definition
of who we are

In their own confusion, the disciples misunderstood the time when all would become clear to them. They assumed that they already grasped the big picture events and the meaning of Jesus having come from God. Yet, Jesus challenged them: "Do you now believe?" (16:31). Little did they know that the real test was yet to happen. "You will be scattered" (16:32). Their confusion persisted as Jesus predicted his own abandonment and death, and in the next breath, promised shalom to them. This peace isn't passive or sentimental, but radical—peace saturated with energy and vitality. It implies a willingness to be transfigured, even in the face of persecution.

■ Which of the following is most encouraging to your sense of peace.

    a. God knows our weakest and most broken parts, our cowardice and fears.
    b. God forgives the sin and chaos of our lives.
    c. God's loyalty and faith in the human potential never wavers.
    d. Jesus dares to trust and love us without attaching any limitations to that love.
    e. This kind of peace cannot be extinguished by the world's darkness.

Accountability

Peace embodied in shalom leads us through a process of becoming the persons we are intended to be. While this kind of well-being is a gift of God, Romans 14:12 suggests that each of us is also accountable to God. *Me.*

■ How can your small group be a gift to accountability?

■ For what are we accountable?

■ Which of the following aspects of shalom is most meaningful to you today? Explain.

    a. Just political practices   d. Creativity
    b. Health   e. Beauty
    c. Equitable economic   f. Other
       conditions for all

■ In what ways do you currently experience shalom with a special friend?

From the cross

From the cross, Jesus quotes Psalm 22, which states, "My God, my God, why have you forsaken me? Why are you so far from helping me, from the words of my groaning?" (Psalm 22:1)

■ Have you ever seen a child lost in a store or separated from parents at the fair? What is that sight like?

■ Have you ever felt abandoned and seemingly outside the safety of divine care? Explain.

Jesus tells his followers to be of good courage because he has overcome the world.

■ What is there about the world you live in that you are glad Jesus has overcome?

    a. Worry   c. Addiction   e. Grief
    b. Loneliness   d. Anger   f. Other

Consider this

A physician once said, "A doctor and a patient bring quite different 'tools' to the equation called health. The doctor comes to the table with prescriptions, surgery, technology, or some medical manipulation that cures. A patient brings the potential for healing."

"O Lord my God, I cried to you for help and you have healed me," says the psalmist (Psalm 30:2). "He sent out his word and healed them" (Psalm 107:20).

■ Discuss the difference between cure and healing in your own life. Can you be whole and experience peace without being cured?

cure - physical   healing - feeling, knowledge, spiritual

A further look

Read Romans 15:7 and Matthew 25:35.

concupiscense
self-seeking desire = original sin
- what attracts our attention
(SI - bath.suit issue)

While God has created us good and blessed us, we also must recognize and take full responsibility for our brokenness.

■ Which "human" things about yourself and others do you find the hardest to accept? Choose one and explain.

  a. Prejudice   c. Selfishness   e. Other
  b. Fear of change d. Need for power *or control*

"All this is from God, who reconciled us to himself through Christ, and has given us the ministry of reconciliation," says Paul (2 Corinthians 5:18). God's gift of reconciliation and peace that Jesus so freely gives includes expectations of us.

■ Choose one of the following and describe the role it plays in building shalom in our work environment.

  a. Patience   c. Tolerance   e. Other
  b. Forgiveness   d. Respectfulness

Discovery

Not this

John 20:21

²¹ Jesus said to them again, "Peace be with you. As the Father has sent me, so I send you."

Jesus' appearance

This text helps to define the appearance of the risen Christ to his disciples. In it, Jesus expresses his healing peace and the completeness of his love for his followers. Undeterred by the recent abandonment during the time of his betrayal and death, after his resurrection, Jesus offers his peace. He desires for them to have reconciliation in their own hearts and consciences. It doesn't matter that they deserted him. Jesus does not chastise them. He affirms and forgives, but he also assigns them his own vocation or "call"—to speak peace. Through Christ's gift, God's love for the world now becomes their vocation, their life-long ministry.

Jesus' peace throughout and beyond his farewell never expects a world without conflict, or one of escapism or easy solutions. What he does promise is his presence and his gift of shalom. His peace contains richness and potential to transcend emptiness, oppression, and injustice—to bless all human life. He stretches us far beyond the achievements and acquisitions of this world to a richer place of completeness.

Our culture

We live in a culture that has little tolerance for pain and misery. We have invented countless means of avoiding both. Our popular media that would have us believe that if we do everything right—work, exercise, pray, eat right, do good, and so forth—all will go smoothly.

■ Do you think peace and wholeness require the absence of conflict and pain? Why or why not?

Vocation

Discuss as a group.

Christ's gift of shalom is your vocation, your calling to share God's peace on a daily basis.

■ Which of the following activities would you most like to include as part of your vocation of peace? Explain.

    a. Visiting an elderly shut-in.
    b. Half an hour conversations with a child.
    c. Time before day starts to pray for wisdom and discernment in your relationships and activities.
    d. Selecting a favorite food for family member or friend.
    e. Making a date with your mate.
    f. Other.

■ Joy is a natural by-product of shalom (1 Timothy 6:17). Describe a time in your life when you have experienced great joy.

■ Where is joy during conflict and disappointment?

■ Do you need to clear up the negative things in your life before you can experience joy? Explain.

Wrap-up

See page 10 in the introduction for a description of "Wrap-up."

Before you go, take time for the following:

■ Group ministry task

note to June

■ Review

move to ? Coast Guard

Vicki Ben Kari friend twins
green eyed monster

■ Personal concerns and prayer concerns

James sister Suzy

Dorothy S. Emily
arthritis son

Ongoing prayer requests can be listed on page 61. See page 62 for suggested closing prayers.

■ Closing prayers

Daily walk

Bible readings

Day 1
Zechariah 9:10

Day 2
Isaiah 9:6

Day 3
Genesis 12:1-3

Day 4
Isaiah 65:17a-18a

Day 5
Isaiah 57:19

Day 6
Judges 6:24

Day 7
Ephesians 2:14,17

Thought for the journey

Jesus gave his disciples a vocation to speak his healing peace. "As the Father has sent me, even so I send you" (John 20:21). Does he give us any less?

Prayer for the journey

O gracious God, source of all creation, author of all goodness and compassion, create in us hearts that yearn to be agents of your peace. Amen.

Verse for the journey

"Steadfast love and faithfulness will meet;
   righteousness and peace will kiss each other
Faithfulness will spring up from the ground,
   and righteousness will look down from the sky."
—Psalm 85:10-11

2 Peace: An Experience of Grace

The gospel's liberating message of forgiveness is basic for the healing power of God's grace—the gift that shapes our daily lives together.

Community building

Our lives are complex. We can surprise ourselves and others with "hidden" aspects of our character. Sometimes this comes as a pleasant surprise; sometimes not so pleasant. Chances are, when we look within, we see an odd mix of characteristics. Some of those parts appear bright, creative, and loving, while others seem mysterious, manipulative, and questionable. Certain facets radiate strength and integrity, while others beg for healing. We are, indeed, human.

Think of a time when you learned something about a friend's character that surprised you. What about a time when you discovered (or inadvertently revealed to others) something similarly surprising about yourself.

■ Choose from the following words the one that best described your reaction to these disclosures. Explain.

a. Delight   e. Embarrassment
b. Anger   f. Acceptance
c. Fear   g. Other
d. Disappointment

Option

Grace can be described as an unearned gift that has no strings attached.

Think of an occasion when you gave someone an unexpected gift. What was their reaction?

Share a time when you received an unexpected gift. What was that like?

Opening prayer

Blessed are you, O God, you who set us free upon your wings of grace and compassion. Teach us to have mercy on ourselves and others. Amen.

Romans 5:1-2

[1] **Therefore, since we are justified by faith, we have peace with God through our Lord Jesus Christ, [2]through whom we have obtained access to this grace in which we stand; and we boast in our hope of sharing the glory of God.**

New life

Throughout the letter to the Romans, Paul holds up the gospel as God's capacity to offer salvation to all who believe. Paul announces a new life made available to every person through God's saving act in Christ (3:21—4:25), not through our own deeds or righteousness (3:10, 21-24). Paul defines this new life through God's saving righteousness—or justification by faith. In Christ we are declared righteous through the power of divine forgiveness (4:6-7). Through faith, that is, through a reliance upon God's grace (undeserved kindness) and not our own need to control, we discover a whole new depth of peace delivered to us by hands other than our own.

Having already established that justification exists through Christ, Paul moves on to focus on the next point. Here he considers what justification gives Christians—peace. Having our relationship with God restored through the power of forgiveness redefines our present circumstances and our hope for the future. We have the deepest peace of all, peace with God, even in the midst of sufferings. However, living with faith in Christ, those sufferings are part of a life journey that gives us endurance, character, and hope (Romans 5:3-4). Therefore, being justified by faith opens to us a new vitality, creativity, and peaceful accord.

Peace and righteousness

Discuss as a group.

The prophet Isaiah speaks of a condition wherein human beings enjoy true happiness when he says, "The effect of righteousness will be peace, and the result of righteousness, quietness and trust forever" (Isaiah 32:17). Paul also talks about peace resulting from the righteousness of God.

■ How can these characteristics and understandings of peace make a difference in your life?

Choose one and explain.

a. Purity	e. Self-discipline	e. Contentment
b. Virtue	d. Good conduct	f. Personal identity

■ Share a time when you had a particular awareness of peace with God.

Peace of mind

Historically, truly great people (such as Martin Luther King, Jr. or Archbishop Desmond Tutu), whether social, political, or religious leaders, have often not enjoyed much peace of mind. In fact, they usually have known, only too well, their own inner conflicts, and the pain and suffering that surround them.

- Name some women and men who could be called truly great.
- Do you think they were (or are) people "at peace" with their environment?
- What do they have in common?
- Where do you think they find their peace?
- Do you think they are at peace with themselves?

Adaptation or "giving in" is sometimes both necessary and helpful in achieving peaceful relationships.

- When have you had to adapt to something or someone's demands in order to reach a peaceful settlement?
- Have you ever "given in" or adapted knowing that you shouldn't have? How did you feel about it? What was the outcome?

Pain

Explore and relate.

While illness often results in pain, pain is not necessarily a symptom of illness. It is also true that the prevailing media messages of today tell us to avoid pain at all costs. We learn to deny, medicate, avoid, ignore, and hide from pain.

- How does pain play a legitimate part in the human process of healing and becoming whole?
- Describe a time when a painful event or condition caused you to make a change for the better.
- Did you have a sense of God's presence (or absence) during this change? Explain.

Consider this

In Paul's letter to the Ephesians, he teaches them that they have been saved by God, not by any special or heroic deeds of their own (Ephesians 2:8-9).

■ What, then, is our motivation as a Christian to do good?

Rank order the list and then share your first and last choices.

a. To gain God's attention/favor
b. To assure our forgiveness
c. To let Christ rule in our hearts
e. To help others
f. To help us reach our potential
g. A thankful heart
h. Other

A further look

Read Colossians 3:15-17 and Philippians 4:7-9. In both passages Paul encourages a way of life based on peace with God.

■ Which of following relational skills would help you most to reflect the life described by Paul?

Choose one and explain.

a. Capacity to listen
b. Respect for others' opinions
c. Sense of hospitality
d. Posture of openness
e. Genuine concern for our and another's welfare
f. Other

Discovery

Remember, if this study theme is used for more than one small group session, introduce subsequent sessions with a "Community Builder" and "Opening Prayer" and end with "Wrap-up."

Romans 5:10

¹⁰ **For if, while we were enemies, we were reconciled to God through the death of his Son, much more surely, having been reconciled, will we be saved by his life.**

Reconciliation

Christ in death carried with him the consequences of our sin. His single act of grace has reconciled us with God. Notice that Paul never speaks of God being reconciled to us. We were the estranged ones. Now a stunning change has taken place. This change sets us in a place that promises us the gift of peace with God.

ace or reconciliation for Paul means much more than a ces-
tion of hostility or the passive calm that follows a battle. He
ews peace as a fruitful and positive condition of creative
rmony. Peace with God is much larger than a single rela-
nship. It embodies accord within our large environment.
d as creator becomes the source of the Christian's inner se-
rity and ultimate joy (Romans 15:13). This becomes the
ace of God which passes all understanding. God's love and
rist Jesus' mediation of that love to us lays before each of us
immeasurable blessing.

th peace and reconciliation refer to more than a cessation of
stility or the passive calm that follows a battle. They reflect
solidarity with God's whole creation. Believers are specifi-
y called to extend God's message of reconciliation to the
rld (2 Corinthians 5:18-20). This is the basis for the peace of
d that goes beyond human comprehension (Philippians
. God's reconciling and saving work through Christ lays
re each of us an immeasurable blessing.

> Recall a time when you gave something anonymously.
> What were the rewards?

> Read Romans 3:23-24; Titus 3:5-7. Describe the grace of
> God by comparing it to something else of value in your
> life.

forgiveness of debt for 3rd W. Nation

m clearly involves more than calmness and quiet. It in-
s a oneness with and accountability to our whole envi-
ent, including our natural environment.

> ▦ Based on this broad meaning of biblical peace, consider
> the following and pick one that has contributed—or that
> you would like to see contribute—to shalom in <u>your life.</u>
>
> > a. Painting a watercolor
> > b. Teaching a child to identify birds and wild flowers
> > c. Attending a symphony
> > d. Cooking with herbs from your garden
> > e. Sharing personal stories
> > f. Recycling
> > g. Other
>
> ▦ Plan an activity that will allow a young person to experi-
> ence the beauty and regenerative qualities of his or her
> natural environment (a photo expedition, creating a ter-
> rarium, reading a story).

Living shalom

If shalom means solidarity and harmony among people, God,
and the natural environment, then living shalom means valu-

Choose one and explain.

Explore and relate.

23

ing oneself, one another, and all of God's creation. Shalom flourishes within the wholeness of all God's creation.

- ■ The following list consists of things we can easily do that cause disharmony and lack of shalom. Which of these interferes most with your experience of shalom? Explain.

  a. Fill up our calendars with too many activities
  b. Take ourselves too seriously
  c. Overlook the value of gratitude
  d. Work too hard
  e. Worry chronically
  f. Neglect to play our favorite music

- ■ If God asked you how each day you experience God's gift of grace, what would you say?

Discovery

Romans 3:21-25

21 But now, apart from law, the righteousness of God has been disclosed, and is attested by the law and the prophets, 22 the righteousness of God through faith in Jesus Christ for all who believe. For there is no distinction, 23 since all have sinned and fallen short of the glory of God; 24 they are now justified by his grace as a gift, through the redemption that is in Christ Jesus. 25 whom God put forward as a sacrifice of atonement by his blood, effective through faith.

Divine gifts

The gospel, the good news of Jesus Christ, announces that through the grace of God every member of humanity now has access to such life-altering gifts as justification, redemption, making amends, and experiencing release. Righteousness revealed in Christ depends upon faith in God's act of redemption rather than upon our obedience to law. Here redemption suggests an act of ransoming or releasing. Slaves of sin find freedom through God's abundantly generous act in Christ (Ephesians 1:7; Colossians 1:14).

Once justified, the believer becomes part of an extraordinary peace marked by anticipation of future good. This peace finds its meaning not in peace of mind or contrived sentimentality and not even in the absence of dissension. This peace comes from the fullest and most positive Old Testament sense of shalom. It reflects the richness of right relationships implied in justification and all the generosity that flows from it. We ultimately have peace as a result of the life and work of Jesus.

Finally, God's sacrifice demonstrates the gravity with which God views sin. It also reveals how God's love brings about forgiveness (Romans 5:8). Peace with God finds its reward in the removal of the fundamental tension running through all of our lives.

Discuss as a group.

Being whole does not mean being perfect, but being completed. It does not necessarily mean happiness, but does expect growth.

Read Hebrews 2:10;
Psalm 18:30;
Matthew 5:48.

■ Rank the following in importance as they relate to perfect:

a. Faultless   c. Virtuous   e. Religious
b. Complete   d. Moral

■ Which one most/least reflects the biblical use of the word *perfect*? Explain.

"All" and "every"

Explore and relate.

Paul's letter to Rome speaks of the gospel as God's power for salvation to all who believe (1:16-17). He talks specifically about God's saving righteousness and universal concern for "all" and "every" Jew and Gentile (3:9, 19, 23-24).

■ Historically, what is your impression of how the church has chosen to interpret "all" and "every" when it comes to the following?

a. Youth   e. Elderly
b. Single adults   f. Racial minorities
c. Homosexuals   g. Women in leadership
d. People with HIV
   or AIDS

Respond as a group.

Consider this

"The chief work that Jesus came to perform on earth can be summed up in the word *reconciliation*. He came to restore human community.... He came to say that God had intended us for fellowship, for togetherness, without destroying our distinctiveness." —Archbishop Desmond Tutu
"On the Evil of Apartheid"

■ Is it a "natural" or is it a "cultivated" human tendency to seek reconciliation? Explain.

■ In what area of your life do you most want to be reconciled? (For example, self, others, God, creation.)

Wrap-up

See page 10 in the introduction for a description of "Wrap-up." See page 62 for suggested closing prayers.

Before you go, take time for the following:

■ **Group ministry task**

■ **Review**

■ **Personal concerns and prayer concerns**

■ **Closing prayers**

Daily walk

Bible readings

Day 1
Colossians 3:15

Day 2
Philippians 4:7

Day 3
Psalm 29:1

Day 4
Psalm 85:8,10

Day 5
Colossians 3:13

Day 6
Romans 5:9-1

Day 7
Isaiah 32:17

Thought for the journey

The journey toward wholeness expects a journey of involvement, of contact, listening, seeing, experiencing. It calls us to be fully present to life and to one another, allowing the past and the future to take care of themselves.

Prayer for the journey

Lamb of God, have mercy on us. Lamb of God, have mercy on us. Lamb of God, you take away the sins of the world. Grant us peace. Amen.

Verse for the journey

"May the God of hope fill you with all joy and peace in believing, so that you may abound in hope by the power of the Holy Spirit" (Romans 15:13).

3 Peace: In Personal Relationships

Personal relationships must deal candidly and fully with the human penchant for disagreement, intolerance, and the <u>improper use</u> of power and position.

Community building

Violence is one cloth, interconnected threads woven together in darkness. Violence directed at self and others—no matter if it is verbal, emotional, or sexual—fuels the engines of family discord, collapse, and destruction. Violence begets violence among individuals, within neighborhoods, and throughout our world.

Conversely, a community life based on forgiveness and reconciliation begets forgiveness and reconciliation. This kind of community extends itself into the world like ripples from a stone tossed in water.

When the apostle Paul lists the fruits of the spirit (Galatians 5:22-23) he offers a prescription for community survival in an age of violence: love, joy, peace, patience, kindness, goodness, faithfulness, gentleness, and self-control.

- ■ Choose one of these fruits and explain why it is important in bringing shalom into your life.

Option

Do you remember being away from home as a child? Did you miss your home and family?

What about times when you have been away from home and family as an adult? What was it like?

Recall a time when you were homesick.

What were the familiar things you missed?

Opening prayer

Break down, O God, the barriers that divide us—the generation gaps, abuse of power, sickness and disabilities, gender, divorce, resentments and injury. Teach us your ways of peace. Amen.

Psalm 133:1-3

1 **How very good and pleasant it is**
   when kindred live together in unity!
2 **It is like the precious oil on the head,**
   running down upon the beard,
on the beard of Aaron,
   running down over the collar of his robes.
3 **It is like the dew of Hermon,**
   which falls on the mountains of Zion.
For there the LORD ordained his blessing,
   life forevermore.

Family unity

Psalm 133 speaks of the blessedness of unity in family. It represents one of a collection of wisdom material called pilgrim psalms. The writer reflects upon and offers direction for every family who made the pilgrimage to the city of Jerusalem.

Israel's social and religious structure depended on the solidarity of the family. The stability that family provided people also served to preserve their community's customs and traditions. Extended families clung together as one, sharing common goals, ideals and interests. Nevertheless, the movement of the Jews to other lands and a changing economic and social structure worked against the survival of family unity.

The psalmist clings to its value. He speaks longingly of the loveliness and blessings of the family. He writes that blessedness, unity, and joy accompany us as we learn to live together in unity as one family and one shalom community.

Today's changing social and economic structures also influence the quality of our family life and sense of unity. Whether our family consists of a spouse and children, other relatives, or a community of close friends, we know the effects of change.

Discuss as a group.

■ Which of the following do you think most affect that which we call family? Choose one and explain.

   a. Changing economic conditions
   b. Caregivers working outside the home
   c. Stress from busyness
   d. Frequency of moving/separation from family
   e. Quality of leisure time
   f. Anti-family sentiments in our culture
   g. Other

Harmony in relationships

In the Bible, harmonious relationships imply relationships that are grounded in justice.

- Give examples from your life where people had honest disagreements over what was just.

- How do churches in your area genuinely respect justice? compassion? diversity?

  - a. How do they free people from bondage to material goods and security?
  - b. How do they challenge gender stereotypes and violent behavior?
  - c. How do they encourage acceptance and charity towards one another? Give examples.

- In what area of life would you most like to see the church address our intolerance of one another?

  a. Race relations
  b. Violence against homosexuals
  c. Needs of people with disabilities
  d. Needs of the elderly
  e. Needs of children
  f. Domestic violence
  g. Ignorance to the need of pregnant teens
  h. Needs of the poor
  i. Other

Choose one and give an example of what might be done to promote peace.

Wholeness

The call to shalom begins when we learn to seek peace with one another at all levels of our daily life. This kind of wholeness benefits from a maturity in our spiritual life that most of us have yet to experience. Christian community can help us to develop this kind of maturity.

- Name a dozen qualities of a healthy community.

A further look

Read 1 Kings 33-10 and Isaiah 55:6-9.

- What do 1 Kings 3:3-10 and Isaiah 55:6-9 suggest about our pursuit of justice in community?

- What is important to remember when we form our views of what promotes justice and peace?

1 Thessalonians 5:15-19

15 See that none of you repays evil for evil, but always seek to do good to one another and to all. 16Rejoice always, 17pray without ceasing, 18give thanks in all circumstances; for this is the will of God in Christ Jesus for you. 19Do not quench the Spirit.

Be at peace

Paul's advice is to "be at peace among yourselves" (5:13). His letter to the Thessalonians speaks of a committed faith community devoted to its members and in need of protecting and preserving itself from outside social pressures. Paul writes to encourage the church, always expressing his appreciation for their steadfast faith in the face of opposition. His counsel is to encourage the fainthearted, help the weak, and be patient (5:14). In summary, he wants them to remain alert and respectful of one another's needs—increase shalom in their care of one another.

Paul knows that the community of faith has the power to deepen a sense of commitment to one another. He understands that a wholesome interdependence among those we live with and care for encourages forgiveness instead of seeking revenge, good will instead of hostile judgments.

Giving thanks to God lifts our mind beyond self, increasing the potential rewards of God-centeredness. Worship draws families together in a robust spiritual fellowship, which can resist the pressures of culture and reconcile gender, economic, and intellectual differences.

Bringing the wall down

Discuss as a group.

The Holy Spirit moves within us and transforms us into people of trust. Christ's life and death have broken down the dividing wall, that is, the hostility between us, making peace and reconciling us to God in one body (Ephesians 2:13-17).

■ What are some recent signs of dividing walls coming down in your local church or community? In the world?

As the salt of the earth (Matthew 5:13) and light of the world (5:14), Christians are to respond to violence in the rich and constructive ways that Jesus taught. Compassion was Jesus's answer to the woman caught in adultery (John 8:3-11). Not only will I not condemn you, but let anyone without sin be the first to throw a stone, he says.

■ Contrary to the life of Jesus, it is quite easy for most of us to judge others harshly. Why might this be so?

Choose one and explain.

    a. We are fearful of the advantages others might have.

    b. It is too confusing to see life from a perspective not our own.

    c. Our self-condemning thoughts come out in a negative response to others.

  ✓d. The need to feel in control of life by avoiding honest complexities, differences, and mistakes.

  ✓e. A prideful preference for the comfort of one's own experiences and biases.

    f. Other.

Compassion

Deuteronomy 4:31 tells us God is merciful. Luke 1:50 states that God's mercy is for generations of those who fear God. Psalm 103:13 describes God's compassion as that of a father's compassion on his children.

■ What aspect of compassion is most important to you? Explain.

In Matthew 20:34 we read that Jesus, moved with compassion, touched their eyes, and immediately they regained their sight and followed him.

■ What are the results of compassion in our relationships?

healing   relating
understanding
acceptance

Consider this

Children in the United States are dying at the rate of about one every two hours in gun violence. Between 1970 and 1991, about 50,000 children were killed.

Parade Magazine (New York: Parade Publications), 9 Oct. 1994.

A related tragedy is the dramatic increase in the number of killings and other violent acts being perpetrated by children themselves. Studies show that early intervention in the lives of children can significantly reduce their violent behavior.

■ **How are children our forgotten neighbors?**

■ **As a group, design a simple activity to be used in the home that encourages compassion in a small child or a teen.**

■ **Discuss what the adult world can do to care more effectively for children.**

Revelation 3:15-16 admonishes the church in Laodicea: "I know your works; you are neither cold nor hot. I wish that you were either cold or hot. So, because you are lukewarm, and neither cold nor hot, I am about to spit you out of my mouth."

What is the opposite of loving? Some would answer hating. But a much larger answer, one that we often overlook, is indifference. Indifference translates to a lack of feeling connected and an absence of caring about what goes on around us.

■ How does indifference prevent the possibility of shalom?

Discovery

Luke 10:29

29 But wanting to justify himself, he asked Jesus, "And who is my neighbor?"

Neighbors

The lawyer's familiar question, "Who is my neighbor?" might be better stated, "Who is the suitable object of my neighborly love?" The answer that follows does not quite fit the question. Instead, it highlights the one who truly bestows neighborly love. So, the lawyer wants to know about neighbor as an object of one's love, and the answer he gets concerns not the fallen man, but the one who had compassion on him.

The priest and the Levite view themselves primarily as priest and Levite (Luke 10:31-32). The man lying at the roadside had nothing in common with either of them. The Samaritan, a layman in religion, would have lived outside of orthodox Judaism, yet he is the only passerby to show compassion. The oil and wine he offers are known from rabbinical sources as curative agents. Of the three, it is the Samaritan who first identifies himself as a human being willing and able to help another human being.

For Christians, the parable underscores the immeasurable depth of our common humanity. To be a member of a Christian community is to stand in a certain relationship to God. A Christian offers a profound affirmation of self by claiming, "God created me and judges; and through Christ, suffered to redeem me." Having said this about oneself, a Christian knows further that the statement applies to every other human.

Respond as a group.

The question, "Who is my neighbor?" addresses a root cause of violence—suspicion of and discomfort with those who are not "we and ours." My neighbor could be unemployed, lonely, lying in need most anywhere along life's roadside; old or young; single or married; black or white; male or female; gay or straight; privileged or powerless.

- What constitutes the goodness of the good Samaritan?

- Why does he make such an inspiring example of neighborly virtue?

Servanthood

He who is least in the kingdom is great, replies Jesus when he discovers the disciples arguing among themselves about who was the greatest (Luke 9:46-48). Whoever wants to be great must be the servant says Matthew (20:26-27; 23:11). Servanthood does not hold much appeal to most people; yet, to serve lies at the very heart of shalom.

- What does servanthood suggest to you?

Choose one and explain.

a. Powerlessness   e. Enslaved
b. Joy of giving   f. Weak
c. Humility   g. Other
d. Affirmation of the
    goodness of life

Consider this

Certain Bible stories reveal less about shalom than about violence, war, and revenge-seeking. The same can be said for church history. For example, we have the just war theory, developed by St. Augustine and used by some people in recent years to justify nuclear war.

Numerous nineteenth- and twentieth-century religious authors published books attempting to establish biblical justification of slavery. We have used the Bible to deny women leadership roles in the church, and even to defend the atrocities of Nazi Germany. The Dutch Reformed Church exercised one of the strongest influences in South Africa favoring the apartheid policy.

- With such inconsistent moral leadership, how can we look to the church for help as we seek peace in our lives, communities, and world?

Wrap-up

Before you go, take time for the following:

- ■ Group ministry task

- ■ Review

- ■ Personal concerns and prayer concerns

- ■ Closing prayers

Daily walk

Bible readings

Day 1
Luke 10:29

Day 2
Matthew 5:43-45

Day 3
Luke 11:5-8

Day 4
Luke 2:48-49

Day 5
Micah 6:7-8

Day 6
Mark 9:35-37

Day 7
Revelation 21:1-4

Thought for the journey

Living as part of a community we begin to see the need for peace in our lives. We are encouraged to see beyond our own pettiness, beyond our tendency to complain and demand that things be done our way.

Prayer for the journey

Break down, O God, the barriers that divide us from one another, the limitations built on anger, separation, gender, and power. Teach us to create not destroy; build up rather than tear down. In Jesus' name. Amen.

Verse for the journey

"Then I saw a new heaven and a new earth; for the first heaven and the first earth had passed away, and the sea was no more (Revelation 21:1).

4 Peace: A Hope for Nations

Focus

Peace on earth, a vision for all nations, seeks to settle discord without violence and begs that the energy of hostility be converted to the energy of compassion and justice.

Community building

We covet peace on our planet and are abhored at the proliferation of violence between individuals, between peoples, and between nations. It can seem impossible for an individual to have any effect, to help things change for the better; but it can and does happen. Recall the song that says, "Let there be peace on earth, and let it begin with me."

■ Select a personal quality from the following list and share how you would like to offer peace on earth through that quality.

a. Flexibility   e. Forgiveness
b. Creativity   f. Hope
c. Compassion   g. Patience
d. Trust   h. Other

Option

Share an event in your lifetime that you see as a moment when the world was blessed with peace.

Think of an time before you were born when there was peace.

What peace can you envision for the future?

Opening prayer

Give to each of us, O God, the capacity for true love that begins with you. Let us be instruments of your grace and peace in all that we do and say. Amen.

Micah 4:3

3 **He shall judge between many peoples,
and shall arbitrate between
strong nations far away;
they shall beat their swords into plowshares,
and their spears into pruning hooks;
nation shall not lift up sword against nation,
neither shall they learn war anymore.**

Social justice

Micah, a prophet who lived in turbulent times, fiercely championed the causes of social justice. He spoke convincingly of the promise of social restoration and his hope for a future world filled with truth, righteousness, and accord.

Micah 4:1-8 expresses the prophet's optimism and expectation of Israel's restoration from exile, the rebuilding of Jerusalem, and an era of universal peace. In verse 3, he speaks of a world in which no earthly ruler would reign. Rather it will be some kind of world commonwealth over which God will reign. God will then bring into subjection all those who throughout history have plagued humankind with troubles.

Micah 4:3 remains today the classic call for disarmament. It presents a picture of the dark and destructive tools of war undergoing a transformation into creative and constructive tools that nurture life and growth. Verse 4 paints a picture of the personal peace and security that follow. In this new world, each person will enjoy freedom from fear and persecution.

Discuss as a group.

- Name a single conflict (social or political) in the past 100 years that has spawned fear, confusion, disillusionment, and finally, a public yearning for peace.

- Which of the following played a pivotal role in that event?

  a. Power   e. Gender
  b. Politics   f. Economics
  c. Religion   g. Other
  d. Race

- What were the "swords" and "spears" used in the conflict? How could they have been transformed into creative and constructive tools of peace?

Consider this

Hope defies boundaries. It has little to do with desires and aspirations. It is larger and more courageous than wishes. Hope works and waits, patiently, willingly, expectantly, always anticipating future good. It never predicts all the answers or demands exact outcomes. It risks letting go. It risks ambiguity, confusion, and even pain. Hope invites us to say our own name and walk our own path. It is sustained by our refusal to acknowledge misery as an acceptable option.
From *Windows on Wisdom* by Mary Farr, 42.
Copyright © 1992 Wordwise. Used by permission.

■ **Share a hope you have for children.**

Renewed hope

The prophet Jeremiah describes God as having plans for humanity's welfare and not for harm, "to give you a future with hope" (Jeremiah 29:11). To hope, then, seems to suggest that the future can be changed, renewed with the energy of compassion and justice.

■ Which of the following do you think would contribute most to a renewed sense of hope in our country? Explain.

a. More/better employment opportunities
b. Reduction of crime
c. Improved schools
d. Stronger family structures
e. More leisure time
f. Clearer values
g. Other

■ How can your choice be seen as the work of God?

The source of much depression and discord is loss of hope. For example, those who work in homeless shelters rife with violence and disorder often speak of a "subculture of hopelessness."

■ Have you ever met someone who had no hope? Explain.

■ Talk about your biggest hope. Have there been times when you have lost hope or had your hopes dashed?

■ What do you hope most for your children or for young people with whom you interact?

■ Consider the meaning of *hopeful*. Which of the following characteristics most/least describes being hopeful?

a. Creative	d. Encouraging	f. A change agent
b. Optimistic	e. Naive	h. Other
c. Positive	f. Strong character	

- Can you think of a person in your own life who exemplifies one of the qualities just listed? Describe that person and what she or he contributed to your well-being.

Discuss as a a group.

- Review the following shalom values and concepts we have already discussed. Which of these run against the grain of today's culture? Explain.

    a. Serving others
    b. Sharing wealth
    c. Feeding the hungry
    d. Taking responsibility for our behavior
    e. Making amends for our mistakes

- What instruments of violence would you most like to see reshaped into instruments of peace?

    a. Intimidating glances   d. Silence
    b. Sarcasm   e. Gossip
    c. Demeaning remarks   f. Other

Discovery

Luke 1:50-53

50 **His mercy is for those who fear him**
    from generation to generation.
51 **He has shown strength with his arm;**
    he has scattered the proud in
        the thoughts of their hearts.
52 **He has brought down the powerful**
        from their thrones,
    and lifted up the lowly;
53 **he has filled the hungry with good things,**
    and sent the rich away empty.

God's reign

Micah's hope for the future of God's reign and shalom also finds expression in the New Testament, particularly in the words of the Magnificat, Mary's hymn of praise following the announcing of Jesus' birth (Luke 1:46-55). The Magnificat declares the greatness of God. The reign of God of which Mary sings closely resembles the one envisioned by the prophets, one marked by peace and justice.

In addition to relief for the needy and powerless comes the wish for Israel to be released from its enemies. Following this deliverance, the Messiah promises to instill faithfulness and obedience to God (Luke 1:68-79).

Discuss.

To seek shalom is to cleanse ourselves of that which holds us back or stands in the way of peace and reconciliation. This means becoming our better selves, individually, and as members of our various communities.

■ What is it about the Magnificat that opens our lives to this peace?

A sense of harmony grows with our ability to appreciate the presence of God in the everyday. Shalom means celebrating the memory of our past and preserving the wisdom that it gives to today and to the new ordering of our lives. It also signals "breakthrough." When we find peace we are released from our "enclosures" and able to love more fully.

■ Describe a time in your life when you had a significant "breakthrough."

■ How did it change you?

■ How could it be seen as a gift of God?

■ If a sacrament is an outward and visible sign of God's saving presence, which of the following would you consider sacramental aspects of your life.

a. Special friendship   d. Sharing a meal
b. Solitude   e. Taking a nature walk
c. Birth of a child   f. Other

Diversity

See Romans 10:12; Galatians 3:28; and Colossians 3:11.

Paul speaks of there being no distinction between people. *Everyone* and *all* are welcome into the community of believers. Yet historically and in our sinful humanity, we don't much like diversity. Instead, we tend to like sameness. We too easily understand peace through sameness.

Choose one and explain.

■ What is it we like about sameness?

■ What is to be gained by appreciating diversity?

■ What makes it difficult to negotiate conflicting viewpoints in a community?

a. It's time consuming to negotiate
b. People don't like to compromise
c. Some ideas are bad ones and don't deserve consideration
d. Negotiating tends to dilute good ideas
e. People don't like to face conflict at all
f. Other

Consider this

It's impossible to do much or learn much about shalom if we don't first listen. We can't love if we don't listen. We can't serve until we have listened to another's need. We can't heal until we let our heart speak to us about its pain and unfulfillment.

Between now and the next session, ask yourself the following questions, listen to your thoughts and feelings, and record your responses in a private place.

■ Where are you on your life's journey?

■ What are your life goals?

■ What "pains" you or keeps you from health?

■ What would you still like to say or do in your life?

■ Describe your deepest yearnings.

Consider sharing your reaction to the experience with the rest of the group.

Discovery

Matthew 12:18-21

18 "Here is my servant, whom I have chosen,
   my beloved, with whom my
     soul is well pleased.
I will put my Spirit upon him,
   and he will proclaim justice
     to the Gentiles.
19 He will not wrangle or cry aloud,
   nor will anyone hear his voice
     in the streets.
20 He will not break a bruised reed
   or quench a smoldering wick
until he brings justice to victory.
21   And in his name the Gentiles will hope."

God is near

Matthew's Gospel serves as a basis for the life of the church. Matthew is the only gospel that uses the word *church* (16:18; 18:17).

Jesus teaches that God is near; God's response to human pain and suffering is solidarity with us. The loving presence of God will ultimately triumph, even in the face of chaos and darkness.

Chapter 12 provides the core of Matthew's Gospel. Here he speaks of the reign of God and how this gives hope for lives in search of identity, purpose, healing, and salvation.

Simple people

Jesus personifies the gentleness that describes the servant prophesied by Isaiah and quoted in Matthew 12:18-21. Jesus chose a simple fisherman like Peter on which to build his church (Matthew 16:18). Jesus gave thanks to his father for revealing the mysteries of the kingdom of heaven to infants instead of the wise and understanding (Matthew 11:25). Jesus blessed the humble, the grieving, the needy, the persecuted, and those who pursue peace, justice, mercy, and faithfulness (see Matthew 5:3-12). Jesus identified the reign and justice of God with concern for human need.

- Who teaches us about justice in our world? The court system? The media? Our schools? The church?

- Consider the following popular understandings of justice:

    a. Justice is blind
    b. Justice is defined by laws
    c. Justice is objective without emotion
    d. Justice is individualistic

  Now consider the biblical meaning of justice and pick the ones that most clearly describe the kind of justice you want for the world (a through h).

Choose one or more and explain.

    e. Justice is seeing
    f. Justice is passionate
    g. Justice is never detached or apathetic
    h. Justice has a social emphasis

A further look

Read 1 Corinthians 13:13 and Romans 12:12.

Love hopes all things (1 Corinthians 13:13); be joyful in hope (Romans 12:12).

There is an earthly realism in the conviction that we ought to make the most of the present moment—to live one day at a time, as the Alcoholics Anonymous saying goes. The ability to live creatively in the present is a sign of emotional wholeness.

Christianity echoes this commitment to the present. In the Gospels we often hear Jesus challenging us to be watchful and sensitive to the possibilities of this hour and of this day.

Wrap-up

Before you go, take time for the following:

- ■ Group ministry task

- ■ Review

- ■ Personal concerns and prayer concerns

- ■ Closing prayers

Daily walk

Bible readings

Day 1
Isaiah 1:17

Day 2
Isaiah 40:30-31

Day 3
Matthew 10:12-13

Day 4
Matthew 10:34-39

Day 5
Leviticus 19:17-18

Day 6
Mark 9:50

Day 7
Isaiah 42:1

Thought for the journey

Jesus says, "You are the light of the world." You are not *like* the light, but you *are* the light.

We don't have to be something extraordinary. We just have to be a light.

Prayer for the journey

In you, O God, we put our trust. May peace break forth as the shimmering light of a new day. May that day come soon. Amen.

Verse for the journey

"He has filled the hungry with good things, and sent the rich away empty" (Luke 1:53).

5 Peace: A Vision for Creation

Focus

The vision of shalom in nature is an invitation for the people of God to be sensitive to issues of ecology and the entire created order.

Community building

Option

At our point in history we can see how recklessly we have treated God's creation and how we have upset nature's equilibrium.

In the name of progress and prosperity, we have denuded forests, poisoned lakes with pesticides, pumped underground aquifers dry, and witnessed the extinction of a shocking number of species.

Share a time when you have experienced the power of nature, such as a tornado, storm, or earthquake.

What did it feel like to witness such power?

Human history abounds with creation myths. Almost every society—from Greek to Chinese to Native American—has its story of the earth and its origins. Many viewed the earth as a fertile mother who gave birth to life. Certain elements of nature were endowed with divinity and ruled over humankind.

The Bible begins with God's work of creation. The earth, the sea, the stars, and everything else are not portrayed as gods or as something to be feared, but as the beautiful and good work of our caring creator (Genesis 1–2).

- Share a favorite memory you have of creation's beauty.

- What part of God's creation would you like to visit that you have not seen yet? Explain.

Opening prayer

Creator God, at your command all things came to be: the vast expanse of interstellar space, galaxies, suns, the planets in their courses, and this fragile earth, our island home. Amen.

Adapted from *The Book of Common Prayer*
(New York: The Church Hymnal Corporation, 1979), 370

Isaiah 11:6-9

6 The wolf shall live with the lamb,
   the leopard shall lie down with the kid,
   the calf and the lion and the fatling together,
   and a little child shall lead them.
7 The cow and the bear shall graze,
   their young shall lie down together;
   and the lion shall eat straw like the ox.
8 The nursing child shall play over
   the hole of the asp,
   and the weaned child shall put its hand
   on the adder's den.
9 They will not hurt or destroy
   on all my holy mountain;
   for the earth will be full of the
      knowledge of the LORD
   as the waters cover the sea.

Isaiah's conviction

The picture of such a radically different social order illustrates the depth of Isaiah's conviction about peace. His idyllic picture of a reconciliation between the world of nature and the world of humans symbolizes a state of well-being and peace.

The passage serves a twofold purpose. On one hand, it portrays a hopeful picture of the future, a picture that offers solace to the Hebrews who lived in the turmoil of the invasions and conquests of the Northern Empire of Assyria (located in modern Iraq). On the other hand, the passage outlines a possibility of what an ideal world could be like.

Discuss as a group.

When we talk about the ideal, we come face-to-face with our own imperfections and lack of wholeness. However, the ideal holds immeasurable value. It gives us a goal worth striving for, even though we might never fully attain it. It furnishes us with a mission and purpose (1 Corinthians 13:10).

■ What were some of the ideals set before you as a child growing up? by your family? your teachers? Looking back, what did you think about these ideals? Explain.

a. Realistic   d. Difficult
b. Helpful   e. Motivating
c. Irrelevant   f. Other

- Would you help set the same ideals for your own children or young people whose lives you touch? Why or why not?

- Are your ideals the same today as they were 10 years ago? The same as your parents'?

Consider this

We live in a scientific world. Renee Descartes, a sixteenth-century French philosopher receives credit for creating our modern world view. His system of thinking promoted science and literacy. It also spawned the further development of the printing press, followed by the spread of ideas throughout Europe. Once this way of observing the world became established, people gained knowledge through facts and information. A personal encounter with life and with the earth held little value in terms of facts.

- **Share something important in your life that is hard to "prove" factually (perhaps a feeling, value, belief, or an intuition).**

Senses

Unlike a world of researched, tested facts, Isaiah lived in a world in which he relied on observations through the senses.

- Which of the following senses gives you the most information about reality?

  a. Sight   c. Touch   e. Taste
  b. Sound   d. Smell

- How does this sense affect your relationships with others? with creation? with God?

You may wish to have someone come prepared to share a poem, prayer, or some other means of reflection that helps you consider your relationship to God through our sense awareness.

Since the introduction of science and technology, all other ways of determining what is real have become suspect. If we can't come up with hard facts that say something exists, we are trained not to believe it does. Yet, today we also see attempts to recover some of the *feeling* aspects of our encounters with God and the earth. It is through these feeling aspects that we increase our sensitivity to issues of ecology and all of creation.

■ Share a time when you have felt God's presence in one of the following. Explain.

    a. Music   c. Prayer   e. Art
    b. Fellowship   d. Nature   f. Other

Discovery

Teaching in parables

The parable of the sower finds Jesus coming out of a house and sitting beside the sea. Such a crowd gathers around him that he climbs into a boat and sits there while the people assemble on the beach. He then begins to teach in parables, or stories describing situations in everyday life. Jesus uses these stories to convey a spiritual meaning.

Matthew 13:3-9 (see also 13:18-23)

3 And he told them many things in parables, saying: "Listen! A sower went out to sow. 4 And as he sowed, some seeds fell on the path, and the birds came and ate them up. 5 Other seeds fell on rocky ground, where they did not have much soil, and they sprang up quickly, since they had no depth of soil. 6 But when the sun rose, they were scorched; and since they had no root, they withered away. 7 Other seeds fell among the thorns, and the thorns grew up and choked them. 8 Other seeds fell on good soil and brought forth grain, some a hundredfold, some sixty, some thirty. Let anyone with ears listen!"

The seed and the sower

This parable, like many others, seems to serve as a lesson in horticulture: The writer uses the same familiar images as does the prophet Isaiah in the previous text. They both employ pictures of nature—rhythms of changing seasons, freshness of the earth after a rain, weeds, thorns, and drought. One can only imagine how familiar and comfortable both writer and reader must have been with the earthy examples they lived and breathed each day. What perfect universal tools for teaching.

Written around the year A.D. 80 for Christians who wondered why the kingdom of God was not more conspicuous now that Christ had come, this parable was intended to instill hope and encouragement to listeners. God's word, like the rain, won't return to God unfruitful.

Humus

The word *human* originates from humus, or earth. We are of the earth, we live off the earth, and we ultimately return to the earth. God sustains our life through such elements of creation as sun, wind, and rain.

- Share a time when you felt renewed or comforted by earth elements such as:
  a. Walking in the rain
  b. Lying in the sun at the beach
  c. Sitting in front of a fire
  d. Canoeing on a quiet lake or stream
  e. Other

Gardening

Anyone who has kept a garden or tried to grow herbs or houseplants knows what it means to have a give-and-take relationship with the soil. Sunlight, soil conditions, insects, rain, and temperature tend to remain outside of our immediate control. More often it seems to be a case of "negotiation" with nature to raise tomatoes on the patio or get an African violet to bloom.

Remember a time when you (or a child you know) were in elementary school and tried to grow something.

- What kinds of earth elements played a role in that process? Did you have success?

- Did the experiment leave you feeling satisfied, frustrated, indifferent, delighted, or angry?

- How can such experiences connect us with the gracious God that Jesus reveals?

Read Luke 13:18-21.

Consider this

The Celtic approach to God opens up a world in which nothing is too common to be exalted and nothing is too exalted that it cannot be made common. The Celts have provided the Christian church with a wealth of prayers and poems from the frontiers of Britain. Once driven to the edge of the church and almost forgotten, the Celts took a humble and homely approach to God born out of harsh lives.

Essentially, Celtic spirituality takes common things and interprets them as pointing to a greater reality. So, getting

up in the morning, washing, making the fire, milking, weaving, fishing, and farming—all testified to Christ's presence. Nearly everything that happened between birth and death could become an occasion for recognizing the closeness, the seeking presence of God.

■ Write a short blessing based on some simple activity that you engage in each day. This could be rising and showering in the morning; eating; working; walking the dog; driving. For example: "Bless this home, this morning, this time of day with you in quiet warmth. In Jesus' name. Amen."

A further look

Assign the following texts to individual group members for reading aloud. Each text refers to the earth's natural elements such as wind, sun, water, breath, and fire: Psalm 104:10-11, 19-20, 27-30; Genesis 2:7; Exodus 19:18; 24:17; Acts 2:3.

■ How can these texts promote an increased sensitivity to the needs of the earth? to the presence of God, creator of heaven and earth? to our experience of shalom?

Discovery

Psalm 96:11-13

11 Let the heavens be glad,
    and let the earth rejoice;
   let the sea roar, and all that fills it;
12   let the field exult, and
       everything in it.
   Then shall all the trees of the
       forest sing for joy
13   before the LORD; for he is coming,
    for he is coming to judge the earth.
   He will judge the world with
       righteousness,
    and the peoples with his truth.

Psalms and hymns

The spirit of all religion shines brightly in the hymns its members bring to God in times of trouble, fear, joy, and celebration. Many of the psalms that we read today probably accompanied acts of worship in the temple in Jerusalem.

Psalm 96 illustrates such a hymn. It celebrates God's rule. It serves as a summons to all nations and to the physical universe to join in God's praise. This and other psalms illustrate that at the heart of our Christian tradition, we have spiritual resources that cherish and preserve nature (see Psalm 98:7-9). The sense of wonder, praise, and awe for God's creation is there and celebrated. Environmental justice cannot be separated from social justice, as both are part of God's vision for wholeness, or shalom.

Earthy stories

By all indications, Jesus displayed earthy qualities and was a man who felt very close to the earth. He used earth stories to teach, and earthy examples such as seeds, pearls, oil, wine, grains, vines, and clay to depict the meaning of his parables. His closeness to the earth suggests a connectedness and interdependence between all of the created order of which he and we are a part.

■ What do you find most surprising in Psalm 96?

a. Nature is seen as having human qualities.
b. It is understood that nature is "alive" and responsive to God.
c. The connection between the praise of God and the judgment of God.
d. Humans and the rest of nature give praise to God together.
e. The energetic attention given to the worship and praise of God.
f. Other

■ Choose from the following what best describes interdependence:

a. Helpless   d. Relying solely on another
b. Mutuality   e. Sharing responsibility
c. Feeble

■ "Rugged individualism" is a term commonly applied to American culture. What does this concept mean to you?

a. Strong   c. Independent   e. Solitary
b. Brave   d. Eccentric   f. Other

■ Which concept, interdependence or rugged individualism, best supports the idea of wholeness or shalom? Explain.

■ Which concept best supports the idea of living in harmony with one another and with our earth?

Wrap-up

Before you go, take time for the following:

- Group ministry task

- Review

- Personal concerns and prayer concerns

- Closing prayers

Daily walk

Bible readings

Day 1
Isaiah 32:17

Day 2
Matthew 6:33

Day 3
Isaiah 11:2

Day 4
Isaiah 11:9

Day 5
Romans 15:13

Day 6
Psalm 96:11-13

Day 7
Colossians 1:15-18

Thought for the journey

Peace embodied in shalom incorporates our wholesome, harmonious relationship with nature. This relationship results in celebration of our physical surroundings.

Prayer for the journey

Open our eyes, O God, that we might see you in every aspect of our day, that we might know you in every measure of your creation.

Verse for the journey

"I have set my bow in the cloud, and it shall be a sign of the covenant between me and the earth" (Genesis 9:13).

6 Peace: A Way of Life

Focus

Peace is not primarily a concept to be learned, but a way of life to be lived. It is God who gives the gift of peace and, as God's people, we build up peace by building up our community.

Community building

"Blessed are the peacemakers" (Matthew 5:9). Scripture calls for *making* peace, not just *liking* peace. While most people would agree that peacemaking is central to the life of the church, an understanding of peacemaking seems less clear.

■ Name one thing you would like to do to make peace.

Choose one and explain.

a. Pray for peace.
b. Join a study group on a peace-related topic.
c. Get involved in the political process on behalf of the disadvantaged.
d. Join an action group serving the needs of others.
e. Visit shut-ins or the hospitalized.
f. Be an advocate for the needs of children.
g. Contribute to a charitable cause.
h. Be more aware of the needs of people around you.
i. Other

Option

Share some new insight, conviction, or experience that you have gained from exploring biblical peace with your small group.

Opening prayer

Blessed God, who gives all that is true and enduring, we give you thanks for binding us together in this holy mystery called life. Teach us to live your ways of justice, love and peace. Amen.

Isaiah 55:1-2,12

1 Ho, everyone who thirsts,
  come to the waters;
 and you that have no money,
  come, buy and eat!
 Come, buy wine and milk
  without money and without price.
2 Why do you spend your money
   for that which is not bread,
  and your labor for that which
   does not satisfy?
 Listen carefully to me, and eat
   what is good,
  and delight yourselves in rich food.
12 For you shall go out in joy,
  and be led back in peace;
 the mountains and the hills before you
  shall burst into song,
  and all the trees of the field
   shall clap their hands.

Invitation

Isaiah 55 concludes a collection of speeches. It begins with an invitation to the thirsty and hungry to come and eat freely at the banquet (55:1). It continues with an offer of enduring life. The invitation to eat and drink illustrates a type of literature that talks about the human search for wisdom, a search that ends with the discovery of the real "food" of life. This real food dwells in the covenant or promise God makes to those invited to the feast. It establishes a bond between God and humankind that promises God's life-giving presence and activity.

Beginning with verse 1, those exiled in Babylon and far away from home in Judah hear about God's graciousness and purpose, love, compassion, and forgiveness. This promise of shalom includes provisions for all of Israel's needs (Isaiah 55:1-2). The prophet admonishes them to work for "bread" that endures, the sustaining food that comes from God, not from demanding life on their own terms. It summons them to life to the full in the context of God's faithfulness toward them as heirs of David (55:3). The result of this covenant is renewed peace for the people of Israel, described in the imagery of a new exodus to a verdant land (55:12-13).

In Isaiah 55 (and Proverbs 9:5-6), the meaning of life is in humankind's intentional search for wisdom and obedience to it.

■ Where do most people you know look for the meaning of life?

a. Work	d. Money
b. Significant other	e. Recreation
c. Children	f. Other

■ What are the choices presented to us in our culture that promise "the good life" and yet do not deliver?

a. New car	h. Popularity
b. Right job	i. Personal appearance
c. Physical fitness	j. Wealth
d. Certain diet	k. Sports
e. Family life	l. Travel
f. Right clothing	m. Other
g. Certain spirituality	

■ What false prizes (advertising) of "the good life" do you find most tempting? Explain.

■ What promise has given you joy and peace? Explain.

Power

To experience God's gift of enduring life and peace is to lay aside countless human attitudes about prosperity and success. We see one such attitude in our understanding of how we should use power. Use of power is a timeless issue of great interest to more than kings and presidents. Power plays an important role in our personal relationships, our family interactions, in and around the work of the church. Historically we have found it difficult to choose anything except power.

Money is power. Information is power. Silence is power. Food is power. Oil is power. Aggression is power. Passive aggression is power.

■ How can power serve our life in community? Give examples.

■ In what ways have you used power in your primary relationships? at work? other places?

A further look

Servanthood builds up community and, not surprisingly, finds its expression in many New Testament texts. Choose the word that best describes servant to you:

a. Attend	c. Valet	e. Bondage
b. Enslave	d. Maid	f. Other

■ Why is servanthood an unpopular concept?

■ What role, if any, does servanthood play in building up peace?

Romans 8:6-8

[6] To set the mind on the flesh is death, but to set the mind on the Spirit is life and peace. [7] For this reason the mind that is set on the flesh is hostile to God; it does not submit to God's law—indeed it cannot, [8] and those who are in the flesh cannot please God.

Rescue

Romans 8 specifically addresses the question asked in Romans 7, "Who will rescue me from this body of death?" (7:24). It is the Spirit who liberates, who frees us from bondage to all excesses and self-gratification that stand in the way of our wholeness.

The Spirit of God is referred to 29 times in this chapter alone. The indwelling Spirit brings to us a vitality, or a life and peace regularly associated with a reconciled relationship to God. It is life "in Christ Jesus" (8:1-2).

The contrast of spirit/flesh introduced in Romans 8:4 is expanded in Romans 8:5-13. *Flesh* refers to the person restricted by self-limitations, self-centeredness, and self-sufficiency. *Spirit* characterizes the person open to and guided by the life-giving presence of Jesus Christ. This person has the promise of life and not death (8:13), and peace is one of the rewards of this life (Galatians 5:22).

Discuss as a group.

■ Give examples of what life lived according to the flesh might look like in the following settings:

    a. Family life   c. Charitable activities
    b. Church   d. Other

■ What would it look like according to the Spirit?

The flesh

Paul repeatedly implies that our physical existence is not in itself evil (Romans 6:12-14). In our mortal bodies we can be creative and good or destructive and bad.

■ What are treasured ways you present—or would like to present—your body, your life, to God?

Choose one and explain.

    a. Prayer   e. Holy Communion
    b. Singing   f. Caring relationships
    c. Service   g. Confession and forgiveness
    d. Sermon   h. Other

- Share one way you would like to set your mind on the Spirit for life and peace.

- How would it please God, yourself, and/or others?

Discovery

Ephesians 4:1-6

1 I therefore, the prisoner in the Lord, beg you to lead a life worthy of the calling to which you have been called, 2with all humility and gentleness, with patience, bearing with one another in love, 3making every effort to maintain the unity of the Spirit in the bond of peace. 4There is one body and one Spirit, just as you were called to the one hope of your calling, 5one Lord, one faith, one baptism, 6one God and Father of all, who is above all and through all and in all.

A way of life

The writer, speaking to the Christian community of Ephesians, begins this section on ethical teaching by advising them that the call they have received presupposes a certain "way of life." This way of life envisions personal interactions shaped by humility, gentleness, and patient concern for other members of the community. The root of this way of life is humility, and one of the fruits of humility is a bond of peace that will continue to grow among them.

Unity

A second theme that the writer develops is one of unity, which is not to be confused with uniformity. He associates unity first and foremost with the Spirit. He expects that unity can coexist with diversity. This kind of unity happens when people can be loyal to each other while also granting to each other the freedom to be different and have different opinions. Unity in this context reaches beyond all the diverse opinions—and still recognizes one body, one spirit, one Lord (Ephesians 4:4-6).

The body

One of the most frequently used New Testament metaphors for Christian community is the body. The concept of the human body conveys many truths about community and shalom. Each part of a body depends on the other parts.

No part can function alone. In order for the body to be whole and well, each body system must function harmoniously.

A significant characteristic of the body metaphor is that it is a living, changing organism. It adjusts to heat and cold. It can adapt to receiving more or less food; it is incredibly resilient when we call on it for endurance and strength. When we consider all the abuse we subject our bodies to, we see that they are remarkable flexible and "conciliatory."

Discuss as a group.

■ Share an example of someone or some group that has impressed you—perhaps even surprised you—with humility, gentleness, compassion, patience, or persistent concern. Explain.

Relationship strengths

When we speak about any community, we are talking about a body of individuals that functions remarkably like a human body. It can and must adjust to historical times and events. It needs nourishment to grow and mature. It needs to keep learning, which often includes unlearning bad habits and incorrect information.

■ Which of the following relationship strengths have you experienced recently in the change or growth of a particular community? Explain.

  a. Taking time for one another
  b. Appreciation of each other's gifts
  c. Open communication
  d. Learning through a crisis
  e. Developing commitment to one another
  f. Having a spiritual center
  g. Other

■ In your daily efforts at building up peace in your home or in another primary community, what kinds of topics cause the most discomfort to the "body"?

Choose one and explain.

  a. Accepting new job responsibilities
  b. Political convictions
  c. Racial views
  d. Religious views
  e. Sexual issues
  f. Gender issues
  g. Other

■ How can you resolve these conflicts?

- Share an area of your life that comes to mind when you reflect upon the word, "lead a life worthy of the calling to which you have been called." Explain.

a. Home life	e. Values and choices
b. Work life	f. Self worth
c. Social action	g. Other
d. Church life	

Consider this

We find in Christ's teaching our need to seek simplicity, make peace, purify our hearts, forgive ourselves and others, sacrifice our own lives, and cultivate a sensitivity that cannot rest while injustice prevails.

- **What are some ways in which we can cultivate simplicity in our personal lives? in our communities?**

- We are one body, says Paul (Romans 12:5; 1 Corinthians 10:17; 12:12-13; Ephesians 2:16). We are all one in Christ Jesus (Galatians 3:28).

Choose one of these words to describe unity and explain.

a. Harmony	d. One
b. Solidarity	e. Unified
c. Fellowship	f. Other

- Where in your life do you experience unity the most? Where would you like to experience it more?

- How has this small group experience influenced your appreciation of peace as a way of life in community?

A further look

Read Acts 4:42-45.

The sharing of goods described in this text illustrates a cooperative group of people who live out their understanding of the economics of justice. In this community, Jesus' teachings and those of the church appear to be consistent with one another. Acts 4:44 reports that there was not a needy person among them.

- Is it realistic for us as Christians to provide for every needy person among us today?

- What should be the guidelines?

- Who should we provide for?

Wrap-up

Before you go, take time for the following:

- Group ministry task

- Review

- Personal concerns and prayer concerns

- Closing prayers

Daily walk

Bible readings

Day 1
Isaiah 60:17-19

Day 2
Ephesians 4:15-16

Day 3
Isaiah 53:5

Day 4
Genesis 11:4:

Day 5
Colossians 3:1

Day 6
Luke 19:41-43

Day 7
Acts 9:31

Thought for the journey

It is difficult for us to accept anything different, yet the dynamic Spirit that empowers us to walk forward and grow is the same Spirit that stirs our hearts to seek peace among ourselves.

Prayer for the journey

O God, you reveal in your servants the signs of your presence. Send us out in the spirit of shalom so that in companionship with one another, we may enjoy your abounding peace. Amen.

Verse for the journey

"Blessed is the king who comes in the name of the Lord! Peace in heaven, and glory in the highest heaven!" (Luke 19:38).

Appendix

Group directory

Record information about group members here.

Names	Addresses	Phone Numbers

Group commitments

"Do not be conformed to this world, but be transformed by the renewing of your minds, so that you may discern what is the will of God—what is good and acceptable and perfect" (Romans 12:2).

■ For our time together, we have made the following commitments to each other

■ Goals for our study of this topic are

■ Our group ministry task is

■ My personal action plan is

Prayers requests

Prayers

■ Closing Prayer

Lord God, you have called your servants to ventures of which we cannot see the ending, by paths as yet untrodden, through perils unknown. Give us faith to go out with good courage, not knowing where we go, but only that your hand is leading us and your love supporting us; through Jesus Christ our Lord. Amen.

Lutheran Book of Worship, copyright © 1978, 153.

(If you plan to use the Lord's Prayer, record the version your group uses in the next column.)

■ The Lord's Prayer

Resources

Books

Bellah, Robert N. et al. *Habits of the Heart.* New York: Harper & Row, 1985.

King, Martin Luther, Jr. *Strength to Love.* Philadelphia: Fortress Press, 1981.

Lebacqz, Karen. *Justice in an Unjust World.* Minneapolis: Augsburg Publishing House, 1987.

Trible, Phyllis. *Texts of Terror.* Philadelphia: Fortress Press, 1984.

Wink, Walter. *Engaging the Powers.* Minneapolis: Fortress Press, 1992.

Wink, Walter. *Naming the Powers.* Philadelphia: Fortress Press, 1984.

Wink, Walter. *Unmasking the Powers.* Philadelphia: Fortress Press, 1986.

Wolterstorff, Nicholas. *Until Justice and Peace Embrace.* Grand Rapids, Mich.: William B. Erdmans Publishing Company, 1983.

Yoder, Perry B. *Shalom: The Bible's Word for Salvation, Justice, and Peace.* Newton, Kan.: Faith and Life Press, 1987.

Please tell us about your experience with INTERSECTIONS.

4. What I like best about my INTERSECTIONS experience is

5. Three things I want to see the same in future INTERSECTIONS books are

6. Three things I might change in future INTERSECTIONS books are

7. Topics I would like developed for new INTERSECTIONS books are

8. Our group had _____ sessions for the six chapters of this book

9. Other comments I have about INTERSECTIONS are

_____

Thank you for taking the time to fill out and return this questionnaire.

- - - - - - - - - - - - - - - - - - FOLD CARD IN HERE, SEAL WITH TAPE, AND MAIL TODAY! - - - - - - - - - - - - - - - - - -

Please check the INTERSECTIONS book you are evaluating.

☐ Following Jesus   ☐ Death and Grief   ☐ Men and Women
☐ The Bible and Life   ☐ Divorce   ☐ Peace
☐ Captive and Free   ☐ Faith   ☐ Praying
☐ Caring and Community   ☐ Jesus: Divine   ☐ Self-Esteem
                             and Human

Please tell us about your small group.

1. Our group had an average attendance of _____.

2. Our group was made up of
   _____ Young adults (19-25 years)
   _____ Adults (most between 25-45 years)
   _____ Adults (most between 45-60 years)
   _____ Adults (most between 60-75 years)
   _____ Adults (most 75 and over)
   _____ Adults (wide mix of ages)
   _____ Men (number) and _____ women (number)

3. Our group (answer as many as apply)
   _____ came together for the sole purpose of studying
          this INTERSECTIONS book.
   _____ has decided to study another INTERSECTIONS book.
   _____ is an ongoing Sunday school group.
   _____ met at a time other than Sunday morning.
   _____ had only one facilitator for this study.

BUSINESS REPLY MAIL
FIRST-CLASS MAIL   PERMIT NO. 22120   MINNEAPOLIS, MN

POSTAGE WILL BE PAID BY ADDRESSEE

Augsburg Fortress
ATTN INTERSECTIONS TEAM
PO BOX 1209
MINNEAPOLIS MN 55440-8807

Not Oct. 19